Why the critics loved
Elegant and Easy Rooms

"Author Dylan Landis gives you the skinny on design: why you shouldn't choose paint from a paint chip, how the right curtains can make a ceiling look higher, what you should spend on a rug, why objects on a mantel should be of varying heights, and on and on. Tightly written and filled with whimsical illustrations, *Elegant and Easy* is a must read for do-it-yourself design mavens."

—Newsday

"If the choicest thing in your apartment is the rattan blinds, don't call in the wrecking ball just yet. Instead, follow these tips from Dylan Landis . . . and give your living space a face-lift."

—Cosmopolitan

"The secrets are short, real, and very good. . . . How to dress a dormer window, how to heighten a room with pictures, variations on an 'endless hallway'—are just a few of the myriad topics that are wonderfully easy to understand, and fast to read."

—Victorian Homes

"Truly helpful hints for spaces large and small."

—The Washington Post

"What it promises . . . this paperback delivers . . . writer Dylan Landis . . . has an inside track to the best professional advice—covering everything from problem rooms to the art of display."

—Better Homes and Gardens Decorating Magazine

Books by Dylan Landis

Metropolitan Home: American Style
Elegant and Easy Rooms
Elegant and Easy Bedrooms
Elegant and Easy Living Rooms
Designing for Small Homes
Checklist for Your New Baby
Your Healthy Pregnancy Workbook
Your Healthy Child's Medical Workbook
Your Health & Medical Workbook

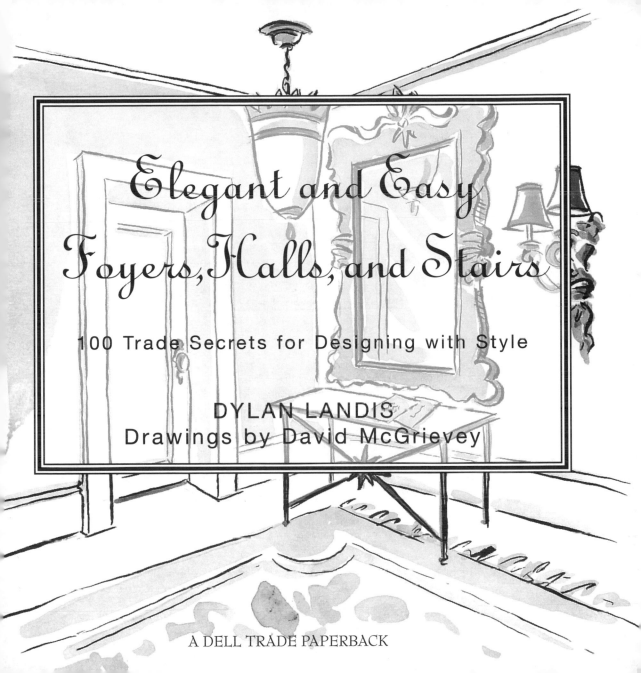

Elegant and Easy
Foyers, Halls, and Stairs

100 Trade Secrets for Designing with Style

DYLAN LANDIS
Drawings by David McGrievey

A DELL TRADE PAPERBACK

A DELL TRADE PAPERBACK
Published by
Dell Publishing
a division of
Random House, Inc.
1540 Broadway
New York, New York 10036

Dell books may be purchased for business or promotional use or for special sales. For information please write to: Special Markets Department, Random House, Inc., 1540 Broadway, New York, NY 10036.

DTP and the colophon are trademarks of Random House, Inc.

Library of Congress Cataloging-in-Publication
Landis, Dylan, 1956–
Elegant and easy foyers, halls, and stairs: 100 trade secrets for designing with style / Dylan Landis; drawings by David McGrievey.
p. cm.
ISBN 0-440-50860-6
1. Entrance halls. 2. Halls. 3. Staircases. 4. Interior decoration—History—20th century. I. Title.
NK2117.E5 L36 2000
747.7'9—dc21
99-045838

Printed in the United States of America

Published simultaneously in Canada

April 2000

10 9 8 7 6 5 4 3 2 1

FFG

For Erica Landis

ACKNOWLEDGMENTS

The best part of writing the Elegant and Easy books was discovering, again and again, how generous designers can be with their hard-won trade secrets. Those named on these pages were also generous with their time, making it a challenge to single anyone out—but I am particularly grateful to Kim DePole, Christopher Fox, and Barbara Southerland for providing an abundance of ideas, and to Barry Goralnick, architect and friend, who taught me much about good design.

Kenneth X. Charbonneau of Benjamin Moore shared his expertise on color. Neil Janovic of Janovic/Plaza Decorating Centers fielded my questions about paint. Erica Landis and Dean Baquet, both passionate about decorating, improved the manuscript with their thorough readings. And David McGrievey gave the book charm and spirit through his drawings.

My warmest thanks, as always, go to my literary agent, Dominick Abel. And I am fortunate to have worked with two terrific editors at Dell—Mary Ellen O'Neill, who launched the Elegant and Easy series, and Kathleen Jayes, who wrapped it up.

CONTENTS

Elegant and Easy
Foyers, Halls, and Stairs

100 Trade Secrets for Designing with Style

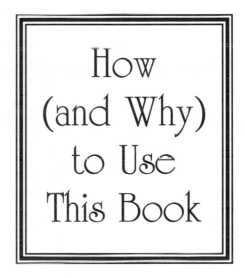

How
(and Why)
to Use
This Book

$\mathcal{B}$elieve it or not, your home is full of extra space, but you probably haven't spotted it yet because of the utilitarian packaging.

I'm talking, of course, about foyers, halls, and even staircases—the transitional spaces that serve as bridges between your "real" rooms.

Because they aren't destination spots, few people truly include these slices of square footage in their design plans. We underrate them, and as a result, we underdecorate them, too.

Consider the typical foyer: It's painted white because white seems a safe and conservative choice; and the furnishings are perhaps a bit stiff, so as to make a "proper" first impression.

But how much sense does this restraint really make? A foyer is a kind of architectural handshake, or greeting. It should create a sense of arrival, generate a little excitement, make visitors (and you) feel supremely welcome.

Similarly, most staircases are painted white, hung with a picture or two, and left alone. As for halls, they are frequently so small, quirky, or tunnel-like that we again decorate with halfway measures.

In truth, these are our forgotten rooms.

The late, great designer Mark Hampton knew it when he ran skinny bookshelves, a mere 8 inches deep, down the length of a long hall. Instantly, he had created an elegant custom library.

And New York designer Alma Nugent knew it when she turned a staircase landing into a meditation spot with an upholstered bench, a small fountain, and a row of votive candles.

A transition space—a forgotten room—is a powerful mood-setter. *Use it*. A room where you spend just fifteen or thirty seconds at a time is the perfect place to create impact and express yourself.

Imagine, for instance, a little entry hall. Now, in your mind's eye, imagine it painted a rich, dark red. It envelops you like a cloak, doesn't it? The color creates an instant welcome, reveals your sense of confidence (even if you doubt it yourself), and makes passionate promises about the rooms to come.

Even better, you're so busy noticing the color that it never occurs to you how small the foyer really is.

The lesson is not about red walls, of course. It's about lining your forgotten rooms with things that matter to you: books, textiles, artwork, candlelight, the sound of running water, a bench upholstered in leopard-print fabric. It's about realizing that all of your square footage, however transitional or vestigial some of it may appear, exists to please you, express your inner spirit, and serve you in some way.

Best of all, beautiful halls, foyers, and stairs are not hard to achieve. The tips in this book—those that draw you in, at least—can help guide your design decisions.

WHAT'S THE DIFFERENCE BETWEEN A FOYER AND A HALL?

Location, location, location.

A foyer is the space into which your front door opens. It's an airlock between the act of arrival and the act of settling in. If your front door opens into an actual hallway, as in many New York apartments, that's your entry hall, another form of foyer.

A hall lies in the interior of the home. Visitors may use it, but compared to the foyer it's a semiprivate space, and you may choose to decorate it in a more personal way.

Many of the tips in this book can be applied to foyers *or* halls, so read both sections for maximum inspiration.

WHO DREAMED UP THESE DESIGN IDEAS?

Most of the 100-plus tips, inspirational ideas, and tricks of the trade on these pages come from interior designers around the country. As a fan (and a design writer), I've spent the last decade quizzing them on the details of their work.

From all those interviews come the nuggets of design advice that pack this book. Indeed, all the designers mentioned in these pages were incredibly generous with their knowledge, and just as specific. (They had to be. If a designer recommended, say, staircase walls the color of eggplant but wouldn't name-drop her favorite paint shade, out she went. Because what good is advice that you can't take to the store?)

Still, there's a caveat: Occasionally, one tip seems to contradict another. That's because designers often disagree. For every decorator who loves light peach-colored foyers with pretty French side chairs, there's another who leans toward chocolate-colored walls, or hangs rusted farm implements as art. Besides, what looks glamorous in some homes may feel impractical in others.

Trust your own instincts: just follow the tips that feel right for you.

THE ELEGANT AND EASY PREMISE

The Elegant and Easy approach to foyer, hall, and stairway design is both forgiving and intuitive. It lets you decorate naturally and impulsively, as inspiration strikes (or as money flows in). It encourages you to trust your instincts, tune in to color, and borrow ideas from the experts. It prompts you to spend money wisely, but also to save money creatively.

That's the premise. Here's the promise:

If you try any five ideas from these pages, you will love your foyer (or hall, or staircase) more.

It doesn't matter if your budget runs to $500 or $50,000, or if you live in an apartment or a house. Any five of these professional design "recipes," chosen from your heart and applied in any order, will make your foyer, hall, or stairs more comfortable, more sensual, more polished, or more vibrant—more of anything you wish, because *your* taste and *your* instincts are the guiding star.

Here's what you won't need: grand plans, floor plans, or exquisitely educated taste. (That's how professionals work, but this book wasn't written for them.)

And let's be honest—here's what you won't get: halls lined in marble and floating limestone stairs, so magnificent that magazine scouts knock on your door. That's because you're probably not rich and (even more important) not a professional.

But you *can* give these transitional spaces and forgotten rooms an Elegant and Easy upgrade.

THE GOAL OF FANTASY

Tradition and formality have their place in serious or public rooms. But when you decorate a hall, foyer, or stair, you're dealing only with a passageway—a place to pause, a sliver of space. An architectural moment, so to speak. If ever there was a place to take decorating risks, get artistic, or try out some gorgeous, saturated color, *this is it*.

Indulge your cravings here. Murals that might overwhelm a bedroom can turn a hall into a tiny slice of Italian villa. Eccentric furniture also has its place, like the cabinets designed for Victorian-era halls—tall, skinny, slightly overwrought in their carvings, and studded all over with mirrors and shelves.

Even extravagant wallpaper that's too wild, or too expensive, for the living room can make a little foyer feel like the inside of a jeweled box.

Finally, *indulge your sense of fantasy.* (Designers do; you'll meet two in these pages who've painted their own halls or foyers black.) You can sheathe a hall in books, create a personal altar on a stair landing, let visitors autograph the walls, or paint the riser of each stair a different shade of blue.

After all, you're just passing through.

CHAPTER 1

Foyers:
Expressive
Walls and
Ceilings

A foyer should be an instant, warm greeting," says Chicago designer Janet Schirn, "and the easiest way to achieve that is with color." Painting your walls something more compelling than landlord white, she says, turns your foyer into a personal and expressive statement. What better way to welcome friends into your home?

Your best bet: Don't play it too safe. If you are going to be esthetically courageous in just one place, that place is here. "An entrance hall is a first impression, so whether it's brilliantly colored or spare and neutral, make it dramatic," says designer Barbara Southerland.

In general, there are two schools of thought on foyers, and you'll probably find yourself drawn to one or the other:

Light, bright, and welcoming. Yellow, after all, is the color of hospitality. Foyers painted in delicate or neutral hues, like feather gray or a biscuity beige, fall into this category, as well.

Intense and dramatic. Front halls painted a dark Chinese-lacquer red qualify. So do lighter colors, if they have an element of surprise, such as high-gloss peony pink—which makes you think you've stepped into a flower—or a moody, almost silvery green.

Which is right? Only one—the one that feels best to you. In color and mood, always trust your instincts.

With a diminutive entrance hall, think Fabergé egg. Instead of trying to make it look larger (usually a lost cause), get rid of extraneous clutter, then decorate for impact. The foyers that make it into design magazines are often tiny pockets of space made glorious with violet, red, chocolate, or peach-colored paint.

"Most people say, 'But won't it look too dark?'" says Celeste Cooper, creative director of the Boston and New York design firm Repertoire. "I say, 'Too dark for what? What are you planning on doing there, besides taking off your coat?'

"They say, 'But the space is so small—won't it look smaller?' I say, 'So what? It's just a space you pass through on your way to somewhere else.'"

<hr />

A note on paint

The most practical paint is latex, not oil. It dries fast, cleans up with water, and doesn't offend the environment. Use an eggshell finish on walls, semigloss on woodwork.

Caution: Paint in rich, deep colors, particularly red, is saturated with pigment. When you wash dirt off a wall painted in eggshell latex, the red pigment may lift away, too, leaving a permanent mark.

Here are three solutions, none perfect: (1) Use eggshell latex anyway, because it looks good. Clean lightly with a sponge, which is less abrasive than cloth. (2) Use semigloss paint. It stands up well to cleaning, but you must have near-perfect walls, as the sheen highlights flaws. (3) For imperfect walls that require periodic cleaning—if you have children, say—consider oil paint.

Foyers: Expressive Walls and Ceilings

COLOR PRESCRIPTION

Every designer has some tried-and-true paint shades that look great in many situations. These are from designer Barbara Southerland of New York City and Greenville, NC. The four palettes look almost seasonal, so are named here accordingly—but choose only for love, not by any calendrical logic.

Spring

Foyer walls: Pratt & Lambert no. 1617, Lime Glimmer, an acidic lime.

Adjoining hall and staircase walls: Pratt & Lambert no. 1616, Seedpod, a pale lime.

Summer

Foyer walls: Pratt & Lambert no. 1859, Painted Lady, a rich coral.

Adjoining hall and staircase walls: Pratt & Lambert no. 1831, Macaroon, very pale peach.

Autumn

Foyer walls: Pratt & Lambert no. 2258, Kodiak Grey, a deep, sophisticated taupe.

Adjoining hall and staircase walls: Pratt & Lambert no. 2251, Appaloosa, a delicate taupe-gray.

Winter

Foyer walls: Pratt & Lambert no. 2229, Gravel, a medium gray-green.

Adjoining hall and staircase walls: Pratt & Lambert no. 2244, Pearl White, a very pale gray.

BROODING BUT BEAUTIFUL

A foyer can have a sense of mystery, even theater. Brooklyn designer Corey Nicholas painted his foyer matte black and hung a colored-glass Moroccan lantern from the ceiling. He drew from his collection of antique religious artifacts: On one black wall, a white-painted crucifix hangs alone, dead center; on another, antique rosaries drip from the frames of religious paintings.

Any collection would work, says Nicholas: in lieu of a crucifix, hang a single violin. Or mount shapely display brackets on the walls, and stand a vase or a small framed print on each.

Tip: *Flat black latex paint, which Nicholas used,*
goes on easily and dries fast; unfortunately, it scuffs
and can't be washed. For a washable finish,
the late designer Mark Hampton favored low-luster oil paint.

SUN-STUDDED WALLS

The Outwater Plastics catalog (see Chapter 6) sells little stamped-metal ornaments that can be glued directly onto walls, as if you were creating three-dimensional wallpaper. Choose something classic, like the fleur-de-lis (less than 2 inches high) or the "sun god" (a radiant sun with a face, about 4 inches across), and glue a row of them under the crown

molding, a few inches apart, or at chair-rail height (36 to 40 inches above the floor). You can even space them evenly all over the walls. The ornaments start at 44 cents apiece, and can be glued with a product called Goop.

For contrast, spray-paint the ornaments a different color from the walls; for subtlety, paint them to match, or nearly match, the walls.

Tip: Use snippets of blue masking tape
(which won't peel paint off the walls) to mock up the
height and spacing before applying anything permanently.

❧

A PROGRESSION OF COLOR

In the Connecticut governor's mansion, guests progress from a rich, dark raspberry foyer (Benjamin Moore no. 1336) to a light blue-green library (no. 666) to a lemon-yellow sunroom (no. 358). Artist Bonnie Rosser Krims tracked down the colors, chosen by designer Carlton Varney, for her book *The Perfect Palette* (Warner Books); bright and natural, these are hues worth borrowing.

The Perfect Palette lists—and shows—the exact paint shades for fifty color schemes, making it a good investment if you're thinking of venturing away from white.

GETTING WHITE RIGHT

Certain shades of off-white work so well on moldings and ceilings—no matter the color of the room—that scores of designers return to them on every job. Look at paint chips for White Dove, Linen White, and no. 925, all Benjamin Moore, and simply choose one you like.

Or if you want your moldings frosted with a purer white, try the favorite of Goralnick★Buchanan, a New York architecture and design firm: Benjamin Moore's Decorators White, applied in latex semigloss.

Tip: Decorators White is technically not made in semigloss, but you can ask the paint store to custom-make it that way. If they won't, try White Dove or Atrium White.

❧

THE ELEGANT FOYER

DD Allen, an architect with the New York firm Pierce Allen, loves Donald Kaufman Color paints for their complexity: all appear to be distilled from mist or squeezed from stones. Kaufman makes only a few dozen shades, though others can be custom-mixed. These colors are also so rich in pigments that your local paint store cannot computer-match them accurately.

Here is Allen's palette for a sophisticated foyer:

Walls: DKC 31, a café-au-lait color.

Adjoining hall: DKC 2, a yellow as pale as butter.

Small accents, like the interior of a niche: DKC 26, a mossy olive hue.

Ceiling and trim: DKC 5, a soft white that's neither creamy nor stark.

> *Tip: The full set of thirty-seven DKC paint swatches costs about $55, but rest assured, these are unusual and subtle colors. (The swatches are big, too, at 4 by 8 inches.) The paint is sold by mail. Call Donald Kaufman Color at (201) 568-2226.*

❧❧❧

THE ELEGANT FOYER II

For an instantly sophisticated foyer, here is L.A. designer Jeffrey Goodman's color choice for walls: Benjamin Moore's

HC-86, a deep taupe. "Artwork in white mats will pop out against it," he says. Paint trim in Benjamin Moore's Linen White. For an accessory table, consider something in dark wood.

Prefer a lighter taupe? Try Benjamin Moore no. 514.

ENNOBLE THE CEILING

Indulge in a bit of grandeur: imagine a foyer ceiling of creamy-taupe limestone or dramatically veined milk-colored marble. A fairly simple faux stone ceiling was created by designer Noel Jeffrey at the Kips Bay Boys and Girls Club Decorator Show House. He happened to be decorating a formal living room with 14-foot ceilings, but the idea is perfectly suited to an entry hall with ceilings over 8½ feet high.

Buy very good wallpaper that mimics any pale stone of your choice. Have your paperhanger cut it into 16-inch squares, and apply them to the ceiling. The checkerboard pattern is centered, and the grain or veins of neighboring squares must always run in opposite directions. The "stone" should look quite persuasive.

Tip: Though Jeffrey used 16-inch squares, a handsome size,
your paperhanger may calculate a slightly smaller size
to fit your ceiling evenly.

WRITING ON THE WALL

For an edgy and inexpensive treatment, Chicago designer Janet Schirn suggests inviting guests to sign your walls.

Paint a small foyer white or any light color, place a cup of black markers near the door, and urge guests to sign their names or leave a message on the walls. Over time, the entire foyer will evolve into a combination guest registry, autograph book, and memory album.

*Tip: To avoid huge, blank areas near the ceiling and floor,
provide library steps or a low stool for visitors to stand on,
and paint a dado (a band of color 36 to 40 inches high, starting from
the floor) as a visual support for the autographed walls above.*

☙❧

GLAZE THE HALLS

Thinned paint, applied in layers of different colors, creates a final finish that looks slightly mottled, translucent, and rich. But though glazed walls are beautiful when done by a pro, it's tricky to mix the right colors (paint lightens when thinned) and to control the end result if you're a novice. *Solution:* Buy a recipe from the California firm art•decor and save this special effect for a manageably small space—the foyer.

art•decor offers colors like slate, parchment, burnt copper, and stone, and charges about $20 for instructions that include the names of paint shades, the proportions, and the exact directions for two translucent coats of glaze. The firm will create a glaze recipe to match, say, your pumpkin velvet draperies (about $45).

For a brochure, contact art•decor, 765 Cedar Street, Berkeley, CA 94710; tel. (510) 527-3904.

THE VIBRANT FOYER

Every room should have a touch of red, as Diana Vreeland, the editor of *Vogue,* used to say. Foyer walls can handle much more than a touch, as foyers tend to run small, and red turns a small room into a jewel.

Two reds worth trying: Benjamin Moore no. 1323, a traditional English red favored by Mark Hampton, and Martin Senour's Independence Red. To locate a store that carries Martin Senour paint, not as widely carried as some other brands, call (800) MSP-5270.

One caution: Red paint, which is supersaturated with pigment, can make walls difficult to clean. Rubbing or washing walls painted in a flat and eggshell finish may actually remove pigment, causing discoloration—so if your foyer attracts fingerprints, consider another color.

WALLS OF OPULENCE

When a foyer's red walls are glazed, not painted, they look even richer (and with glazes based on oil paint, they're easier to clean). Glaze takes a flat color and gives it depth, complexity, and gleam. The process is labor-intensive, but here is a straightforward recipe that Austin designer Hortensia Vitali invented and swears by. Her formula yields "a rich, true, passionate red."

Roll on a coat of taxicab-yellow latex paint in eggshell: Benjamin Moore's no. 322.

Mix four parts Benjamin Moore Alkyd Glazing Liquid with one part Martin Senour's Independence Red in flat oil paint. Using a circular motion, rub the glaze on with a small natural sponge, and promptly rub it off again with a soft, clean T-shirt. (Vitali's tip: Copy the "wipe on, wipe off" technique from the movie *The Karate Kid*.)

For the second glaze coat, repeat with Martin Senour's Embers. For the third, use Martin Senour's Moroccan Red. Make sure each coat is completely dry before applying the next.

BRING THE CEILING INTO PLAY

Two-story foyers can look impressive, but height can create a sense of remoteness. To restore some sense of welcome and intimacy, tug the ceiling down slightly by painting it a color that's darker than the walls.

Here is New York designer Marshall Watson's preferred palette:

Taupe ceiling: Benjamin Moore HC-81.

Yellow walls: Benjamin Moore no. 170.

Warm white moldings: Benjamin Moore's White Dove.

BORROW FROM HISTORY

Try rethinking a windowless or cheerless foyer as the entry to a Mission-style bungalow—sober and rich, with deep colors drawn from nature. For walls, dip into the Frank Lloyd Wright collection, which the architect created in 1955 for Martin Senour Paints. Call (800) MSP-5270 for a brochure on the collection and store locations.

Some personal favorites: Oak Bark (FLW-13), Mountain

Red (FLW-24), Green Olive (FLW-16), and Dark Eggshell (FLW-34, a café-au-lait color despite the name).

Newly reissued, these colors look great with the dark oak and sober lines of Mission furniture and reproduction Arts and Crafts lighting fixtures (from catalogs like The Bright Spot; see Chapter 6).

CHAPTER 2

Foyers:
Furniture,
and
Display

𝒜lexandra Stoddard, the author and designer, lives in a New York apartment with an extravagant foyer: it's 9 feet wide, 24 feet long. Under an ethereal sky-blue ceiling, Stoddard parks a huge French farm table, and when she pulls it away from the wall, twenty people can sit down to dinner—in her foyer.

A few blocks away, designers Scott Salvator and Michael Zabriskie have an entryway that feels smaller than a walk-in closet. Yet theirs, too, is an arresting space, lined like a jewel box in lacquered paper. And, like Stoddard's, it is also "furnished"—with a row of antique finials that jut from the wall, awaiting coats.

The point is that any foyer will pay you back handsomely if you treat it like a room. It may not have space for a table, or even a chair. But an architect put it there for a reason. The entryway creates a moment of arrival, a transition from the outdoors to domestic shelter, and even a bit of suspense before the rest of a home is revealed. With good lighting, a mirror, and a well-organized place for coats, you can help it do its job to the fullest.

Moreoever, unless you live in a mansion, a carefully furnished front hall can serve you in other ways. Depending on its size and contents, a foyer can store books, host dinners, even put up an overnight guest. It can show off your collectibles and keep your keys from getting lost. To visitors, it heralds your personal style, whether elegant or artistic or serene. And to you, it offers a genuine sense of welcome every time you come home.

REMEMBER THE TELLING DETAILS

Invest in better hangers for your coat closet. It may be awhile since you've paid for a hanger, but shapely wooden ones, particularly in black, impart functional elegance to the closet—

which is, after all, a place your visitors see up close. Besides, good hangers make your clothes last longer.

CREATE AN INSTANT MUDROOM

If your entry hall closet is crammed with your own clothes and can barely accommodate your guests' coats, turn a large pine cupboard or armoire into a "mini-mudroom," suggest

Elizabeth Gaynor and Kari Haavisto in their book *Stylish Solutions* (Clarkson Potter). This requires a carpenter, who can outfit the armoire's interior with cubbyholes and sturdy hooks. Umbrellas, boots, and overcoats can all be stashed here—yet when the door is closed, simplicity reigns.

Another bonus: A large armoire with some height and breadth to it can scale up a small foyer.

THE FRAGRANT FOYER

The scent of a room can engage you immediately, coming or going. Keep a vase of eucalyptus in the foyer; it smells fresh and natural, even from across the room. Look for young branches, with leaves still small and green, not yet silvery. The scent (and the leaves themselves) will last long after the eucalyptus dries.

UPGRADE THE LOOKING GLASS

Every foyer needs a mirror—large enough so you can adjust your hat, and clear enough (no scarred antique glass) for fixing your lipstick. Buy something with a little history: consider a traditional gilt-framed mirror, a glittering Venetian mirror, or a large Victorian oval mirror.

Tip: A beveled mirror always looks richer.
Remember that any framer can insert a beveled mirror into an
antique or vintage flea-market frame.

ENHANCE A DOORWAY

Emphasize your foyer's most prominent doorway (often the door to the living room) by flanking it with decorative display brackets, two stacked vertically on each side. Place pottery or pillar candles on the brackets, and hang an antique platter or two above the door (using ordinary plate hangers from any hardware store, or decorative ones from the Martha By Mail catalog listed in Chapter 6). Thus crowned, the doorway becomes an important-looking portal, and your good ceramics get displayed as well.

You can achieve the same effect with a collection of small prints or watercolors: hang two or three, stacked, on each side of the doorway, and hang several more above the door.

DRAMATIZE A DOORWAY

New York designer Kim DePole has her own artistic approach to doorways: She uses a hot-glue gun (from craft and hardware stores) to border a doorway with vintage postcards, or antique saucers, or even a mosaic of small squares of any large picture she has neatly snipped up. "It's very graphic, and turns the doorway into an elaborate frame," she says.

Tip: Be warned: Glue is permanent. Tape, or sticky-backed Velcro, may give you more flexibility.

⚜

ACCENTS FROM THE GARDEN

The foyer (at least in a house) is a link between nature and shelter. To make the transition graceful, bring a bit of nature indoors. Mount a display bracket low on the wall—above the hall table or under a framed mirror—and have a rotating display: a potted orchid, a pine cone, a sheaf of twigs tied with raffia, or a Zenlike arrangement of three smooth stones from the beach.

Or frame something from the garden or a nearby park: a feather, two autumn leaves, a snippet of fern. It need not last forever; instead, think of capturing various moments of the seasons. Here's a great method from *Martha Stewart Living* magazine:

Buy two panes of glass with honed edges (to prevent cuts) from a glass supplier, which you can find in the Yellow Pages. Sandwich the leaf between them, and clamp the

Foyers: Furniture and Display

33

panes together with two jumbo binder clips from a stationer's. The clips have holes, so the "frame" hangs easily from a nail. For safety's sake, keep the panes fairly small and the clips large.

LET THE LIGHT INTRIGUE

Replace a plain foyer lighting fixture with an antique. This is probably cheaper than you think: at flea markets you may find cast-metal or crystal-dripping sconces for as little as $30—especially if they've lost a mate—and countless crystal chandeliers can be had for well under $300.

Tip: For safety, unless the dealer has rewired the fixtures already, always take old fixtures to a lamp-repair shop for rewiring.

❧

THE ANCHORING TABLE

Years before the invention of the coffee table, the Victorians planted center tables—which were taller and often oval—in their living rooms. Try placing a round table in the middle of your foyer, where it can hold mail, keys, and flowers, making the foyer a refreshing place in which to pause. For foot traffic, leave at least 3 feet of clearance on both sides of the table.

***Tip:** If you live in an apartment where the front door opens smack into the living room, you can create the effect of a foyer by placing a round or oval table near the door.*

THE GOURMET FOYER

A good-sized foyer can double as a dining area. This can be helpful if your home lacks a dining room (or if you've turned the dining room into, say, a study). The key ingredient is simply a great-looking table, perhaps one with leaves that fold down so it can double as a console against the wall. For dramatic effect, hang a heavy-bodied curtain that sweeps across the front door at dinnertime, so the foyer takes on the feeling of an interior room.

Tip: To curtain a front door, choose a substantial-looking rod and let it extend roughly 12 to 18 inches on either side of the door (so the curtain, when swept aside, won't interfere with the door). Trust your eye in determining the proportions.

❧

MAKE THE MOST OF FLOOR SPACE

Instead of crowding a small foyer or entry hall with furniture, mount a console table directly to the wall, using one large central bracket that reaches to the floor, or a pair, one on each side, that doesn't. By not relinquishing floor space to furniture with legs, you'll make a tiny room look a little more generous, and you'll still have a surface for mail, gloves, and keys.

A WEATHERBEATEN ESTHETIC

For a foyer table with an old-farmhouse patina, Brooklyn designer Christopher Fox buys an inexpensive console from an unfinished-furniture store, then adds paint, wind, and rain. His recipe:

Haul the table into the backyard and treat according to the season:

Winter—Paint with flat white latex paint. Except for blizzards, leave outdoors until spring. It will be peeling and bubbling like a timeworn antique. Have a handyperson tighten its joints if needed.

Summer—Paint a vibrant color, using flat latex paint (see color tip, page 39). Set table in a sunny spot. Dissolve three cups of salt into enough water to fill a spray bottle (boiling speeds the process). Spray the piece daily. The paint will blister, bubble, bleach, and fade by fall.

Tip: For summer colors, Fox likes these from the
Ralph Lauren Polo Sport Collection: Tournament Blue, Anthem Red,
Orion Gray, Catamaran Yellow, or Outrigger Orange
(which bakes to a terra-cotta finish).

❧

CONJURE SERENITY

New York designer Alma Nugent believes that every home needs a spiritual center, "a space where you can pause to appreciate yourself, your home, and the day." In a small apartment or diminutive house, she suggests, why not use the foyer? Here are Nugent's ingredients for a peaceful foyer sanctuary:

- A mirror in which you glimpse yourself immediately upon entering. This serves as a reminder to focus on yourself for a few moments.

- Candlelight. If your entryway has no room for a console table, hang a display bracket on the wall and place a votive candle in a glass on the bracket.

- Running water. In a small space, it might be a wall-hung fountain ordered from a garden catalog (see Chapter 6).

Foyers:
Furniture
and
Display

- A symbol of something important to you, preferably with a meditative air. At the Harlem United Show House in New York, Nugent included a bust of Martin Luther King, Jr., that shows him in a private reflective moment with a distant gaze.

- A bench, if possible, for contemplation.

LISTEN TO THE ROOM

Are the sounds of your foyer pleasing? Change a doorbell if its ringing annoys you. Consider instead a mechanical doorbell (see the Renovator's catalog, Chapter 6), which must be turned by hand, or an antique door knocker (check flea markets and antique shops).

THE DELICACY OF CANDLELIGHT

For a theatrical setting when guests are expected at night, Christopher Fox darkens the foyer light and lines the perimeter of the foyer's hardwood floor with dozens of votive candles in glass containers. (Obviously, this is a potential fire hazard; don't try it in narrow halls or on carpeted floors, around children, or where alcohol is being served.) The glow will illuminate the lower 3 or 4 feet of the wall. "It's warm and complementary," says Fox, "and leads your guests toward the gathering spot."

Tip: Pour half an inch of water into the votive glass, and the melted wax won't stick to it.

꙰

THE FOYER AS GUEST ROOM

If your small house or apartment is graced with a large foyer, you may be able to create guest quarters here. T. Joan Gibbs, a New York designer, pulled this off by furnishing a 10- by -12-foot foyer with a twin-size nineteenth-century Empire daybed. She

dressed it in raw silk and made four large square silk pillows to serve as a backrest. Two side bolsters, also silk, further suggest that this is a sofa—not a bed. Add a rug, and a small table for flowers and keys. "You could do this in a foyer as small as 9 by 10 feet," says Gibbs. For overnight guests, just add sheets.

THE TOO-TALL ENTRY HALL

Some new houses welcome visitors with a two-story foyer that may feel awe-inspiring but lacks warmth. To create a more human scale in one client's 18-foot-high entry, Jeffrey Goodman of the Los Angeles design firm Goodman Charlton hung three paper lanterns at three different heights—approximately 10 feet, 12 feet, and 14 feet above the floor. "They commandeered the empty upper reaches of the space," says Goodman.

He used shades by Isamu Noguchi; these are midcentury icons, to be found at better lighting stores. You can substitute any paper shade that can safely surround a light bulb. Your major expense will be rewiring the ceiling, which requires an electrician.

Alternately, light the foyer with a lamp and suspend three or more Chinese lanterns from the ceiling. They can't take the heat of a bulb but have high decorative value (try Chinatown department stores, or www.Pearlriver.com).

Foyers:
Furniture
and
Display

43

STEP OUTDOORS

When you think your foyer is finished, step outside and look at your front door as visitors see it. Does the door need re-painting? Would it benefit from a brass kickplate along the bottom? If the doorbell, knob, doormat, or the house or apartment number are not objects of beauty, replace them.

Sources: Restoration Hardware and Craftsman Homes Connection catalogs (see Chapter 6).

Halls: Expressive Walls and Ceilings

ℐf you could shrink your hall down to the size of a box, how would you want it decorated? Like an antique French jewel box, or an elegantly lined English hatbox? A serene Shaker band-box, or something handpainted by a folk artist?

The great thing about a hall, however narrow or awkward, is that you can take liberties here. After all, halls are essen-tially private. (If your front door opens into one, it's an *entry* hall and thereby qualifies as a foyer.) A luscious color that might overwhelm the bedroom can make a hallway dreamy and exotic; so can handpainted stripes, a mirrored wall, and many other design fantasies. Remember, in small doses, anything goes.

A little hall is also the perfect spot for luxuries: hand-blocked wallpaper, for example, or even velvet-upholstered walls that would be unaffordable in larger rooms. In a long hall you'd need a pair of sconces for ample light, but in a tiny space you can get away with one—and an antique sconce that's missing its mate will sometimes sell for a song.

Try to resist painting a hall white. Without natural light, white paint can look dreary. And without benefit of other enticements—interesting artwork or an Oriental rug—a white hall risks becoming a dead space in an otherwise vibrant home.

This is why the designer Carlton Varney once advised: "Whatever you do, never leave a hallway in limbo."

One rule, a small one, is worth observing: *Do* paint the hallway woodwork the same shade of white you've used throughout the house. Even if the hall is a complete visual departure from the rooms around it, the matching woodwork will create a subtle continuity that holds the house (or apartment) together.

A note on paint: Some basic good advice and a strong caution appear in Chapter 1. Read before you paint.

CREATE YOUR OWN MEMORY LANE

A hallway is literally a route to a destination, so consider a display of artwork connected with destinations you have a passion for.

- Vintage picture postcards of your home state, or cities you've visited, or places that have always struck you as romantic. Shop flea markets and have oversized mats custom-cut by a framer, but save money with ready-made store-bought frames.

- Frame a collection of vintage and antique maps, or architectural prints, of every place you've visited or lived, suggests Terry Trucco, author of the book *Color: Details and Design* (PBC International). Dealers of prints or old books are great sources, as are flea markets and antique shows.

THE (TEMPORARILY) POETIC HALL

What do you do with a hall that's wallpapered with a design you can't stand? Eventually you'll steam it off. Until then, here's a romantic quick fix—for tiny spaces only—from designer Corey Nicholas of Interior Sense in Brooklyn, New York:

Buy three or four fat old books of poetry. They must be the same size and old enough for the individual pages to show their age. Don't buy anything valuable, because now you're going to *carefully* tear out all of the pages. Tape a border of pages very neatly along the straight edges of the walls—at the ceiling, baseboard, and corners—allowing for some overlap. (It hides the tape.) Now fill in the rest of the wall, taping up pages in a slightly looser fashion, almost as if the pages had floated toward the wall and stuck there. When the wall is completely sheathed in pages, the hall will be exquisitely poetic, at least temporarily.

Tip: Old sheet-music would also work well.
And poetry beats prose, because it looks less crowded on the page.

✵

ADD SPARKLE—AND ART

Confronted with an undernourished little hall—about 6 feet long and 3 feet wide—in their own New York apartment, designers Scott Salvator and Michael Zabriskie gave it the grand treatment. They mirrored one of the 6-foot walls and

"hung" a tall arrangement of prints on the mirror. How? Easy: by applying sticky-backed, black Velcro (from fabric and hardware stores) all around the backs of the frames, and to the mirror. Now the mirror adds dimension and gleam, while the art gives you something to look at besides your own reflection.

The other walls were papered in a beige-on-beige stripe, the ceiling with a beige paper bearing tiny stars. Everything, in other words, was visually quiet, yet rich enough to be used in grander rooms. The moral? No hall is so tiny that it's undeserving of a little elegance.

THE WELL-READ HALL

Turn a hall into a library: build in shallow shelves from floor to ceiling. It won't crowd the space if you remember that a mere 8-inch-deep shelf will accommodate most hardcovers, says Michael Buchanan of New York's architecture and design firm Goralnick★Buchanan. Let the shelves touch the ceiling, then install a picture light above each bay of books. "It's a great way of adding task lighting," says Buchanan, "and it gives a finished look, as if you went beyond the call of duty and did extra detailing."

It helps to hire a pro: work with a skilled carpenter or even a decorator to design the shelves, and have an electrician wire in the lights.

Tip: These shelves aren't furniture;
they're architecture.
Make sure they have baseboards along the bottom and
crown molding along the top.

❧

GIFT-WRAP A SMALL HALL

For exotic wall treatments, explore a paper store, such as Aiko in Chicago or Kate's Paperie in New York. (Kate's has a catalog; see Chapter 6.) Silvery tea paper, rice paper, or various handmade materials can be applied to walls, ceiling, or both by any good wallpaper installer. (The silver tea-paper ceiling is a classic, made popular by the late, great American decorator Sister Parish.) The papers are costly but not excessive for a small hall, or even just the ceiling, and the space could end up looking like the interior of a beautifully lined box.

THE RURAL HALL

If you dream of the countryside, consider colors that seem to be borrowed from a farm: Donald Kaufman Color's DKC 17, a dark barn-red, and DKC 20, a light, mustardy yellow. New York interior designer DD Allen of Pierce Allen likes both in small halls, with DKC 5, a soft white, for ceiling and trim.

Source: Donald Kaufman Color swatches and paint are sold by mail; call (201) 568-2226 to order. You can also examine rooms painted with DKC paints in the book *Color Palettes*, which is keyed to the collection, by Suzanne Butterfield (Clarkson Potter).

THE ORCHARD INFLUENCE

Also terrific in a small hall, according to DD Allen: DKC 23, a bright apple green. For small accents, such as a niche, try DKC 30, a soft yellow. Again, use DKC 5 for white moldings and ceiling.

BROADEN THE HALL

To make a narrow hall seem wider, suggests designer Hortensia Vitali, bring the ceiling color down to cover the top 12 inches of the walls. The ceiling will look more expansive, and your mind's eye assumes that the floorspace, too, must be wider. Try this the conventional way, with a white ceiling over walls painted in a color (either vivid or neutral). But it also works with a colored ceiling over lighter walls—think sky blue over white.

CREATE A TEMPLE

To break up a long and narrow space, designer Michael Buchanan installs pilasters (flat columns), marching them in pairs down a 10- or 15-foot hall. "It breaks the wall up into bays, and makes it easier to display art," he says. An ideal quantity, he says, is six pilasters—three pairs that face each other at regular intervals across the hall. (If doorways interfere, you may have to settle for two pairs.) You can also "install" pilasters around a hall or foyer of any other shape as long as you can achieve symmetry.

    Buchanan uses real architectural pilasters, but you can stencil your own with paint, or apply them as wallpaper.

Sources: For a catalog of architectural stencils, contact The Stencil Collector (see Chapter 6). Or apply Gramercy's wall–paper columns—13-inch-wide Ionic fluted pillars, sold for $25 a yard, plus a separate base and capital ($40). The columns come in white, beige, or taupe; for retailers, call (800) 988-7775. Hire a professional paperhanger, the company advises.

BLACK AS NIGHT

Jeffrey Bilhuber, a New York designer, says black walls are the perfect backdrop for hanging photographs—and that a black hallway makes esthetic sense anyway. "It has resonance, and it gives weight and integrity to all the rooms around it," he says. Instead of pitch-black, he uses Pratt & Lambert's Obsidian, "the color of a match struck." With latex paint, choose eggshell or satin for a slight luster, says Bilhuber.

Tip: The darker your wall color, the smoother the walls must be. You might have to hire a plasterer, so consider this a preparation-intensive job.

✥

THE VICTORIAN CEILING

Make your hall ceiling a beautiful "lid" to distract from the confining space. Have it papered with Lincrusta, an embossed paper much like the tin ceilings favored by the Victorians. (For full effect, illuminate it with a pair of halogen wall sconces that cast their light straight up.)

Lincrusta must be painted, but New York designer

Marshall Watson goes one step further, making the ceiling appear almost coffered: he paints it with Benjamin Moore's Linen White, then applies a light gray glaze (made by stirring several cups of any dark gray paint into a gallon of glazing medium). As he works, he rubs the wet glaze off with a rag. "The gray that remains will deepen the shadows in the Lincrusta pattern," he says.

Tip: When buying paint and glaze, use all oil-based or all water-based products. In paint, as in life, oil and water don't mix.

❧

GENERATE LIGHT WITH MIRROR

Add dimension to a hallway by having a glazier (that's a glass supplier; see your Yellow Pages) apply mirror to the face of the doors. Mirror can be set into a door's already recessed panels or applied to a flat door with wood trim added afterward, as a frame, says New York designer Nan Lee of Lee/Wimpenny. The mirror will bounce light around and add depth, always good remedies for a small space.

Tip: Don't apply mirror directly to a door that faces your front door, as guests' first sight should be of your home, not of themselves.

❧

SUMMON UP AN INTERIOR VIEW

Commission a trompe l'oeil mural, says Marshall Watson. "It won't cost as much as in a larger room—and a small hall bears close inspection, so it's worth the investment."

Your mural could be as simple as tall bamboo plants that grow straight up the walls and into a canopy of silvery-green leaves overhead. Or take inspiration from the underwater mural that DD Allen once commissioned for a client's ceiling; it showed the underside of a boat from which a man was fishing.

A MINI-RENOVATION TIP

To make the rooms next to a little hall look taller and larger, have a contractor lower the hall ceiling. (He or she will actually install a new ceiling, perhaps 8 feet above the floor—no lower!) Paint the hallway a color that's darker and richer than the surrounding rooms. It's an old architectural trick: a strong contrast between two rooms will underscore the qualities of each.

Halls:
Expressive
Walls and
Ceilings

57

TEST COLORS LIBERALLY

Testing paint colors on the walls can get pricey, with quarts costing up to $15. But sources are cropping up for test-sized samples; they not only cost less but make it easy to try colors that might otherwise seem too daring.

- Four-ounce jars of more than 1,000 Pratt & Lambert colors cost $2 apiece, plus shipping; call Adler Brothers in Providence, RI, to order the hues you want; tel. (401) 421-5157. Examine paint strips at your local store first.

- Waverly, the fabric and wallcoverings firm, now makes paint—and sells its most popular shades in tester jars for $3 to $4. To find a store that stocks the samples, call (800) 406-8177.

CHAPTER 4

Halls:
Furniture
and
Display

Whatever its dimensions, a hall should be furnished—even if it can hold nothing more than one pretty side chair, or, if there's truly no room, a wall-mounted shelf holding a vase of tulips. (Here's a floral design tip: Use a wide-mouthed vase, and let the tulips swoon.)

"Furnishings give the hall dimension, so it's not just a tunnel from one place to another," says New York designer Craig Raywood. "They make the hall a room. With a bench or a narrow console table, and some pictures on the wall, you're not just passing by any more. You've made the hall a place to pause."

That's one purpose of decorating a hall—to create a place to pause between rooms, the visual equivalent of the sherbet that the French serve to clear the palate between courses. A second purpose is to indulge in sensory splurges or displays of memorabilia—things too personal for a foyer (which stands slightly on ceremony to welcome guests), but perfectly suitable for the more private hall.

It may be a stretch to think of a hallway as a room, but if you change your attitude toward the space, you can, to a degree, defy its constricting architecture.

For example, if a large hall feels to you like wasted space, give it a job. Look for dual-purpose furniture that doubles as storage. A skinny console table, skirted, can hide your winter sweaters underneath; an apothecary chest, with its myriad drawers, can stash postcards, stamps, overflow from the medicine cabinet. A little writing desk can even turn an empty nook into a miniature home office.

Or consider the impossibly small hall. It may not accommodate a stick of furniture, but it can probably hold wall-mounted ledges or display brackets. Ledges, if deep enough and used in threes or fours, can marshall anything from paperbacks to picture frames. Brackets can hold vases or other *objets*.

Finally, there's the long, skinny hall. This type of interior tunnel is best transformed into a picture gallery. Treat the art well—even paintings by your four-year-old niece will look impressive if well framed—and this hall can look terrific. As a last investment, consider buying small track lights so you can wash the art with light.

FOR YOUR EYES ONLY

Put flowers in an interior hallway, where visitors may not see them—but you will. Because they're unexpected, you'll appreciate them more.

In a hall with no table, check home accessory or floral design stores for a wall vase, a removable glass container supported by a wall-mounted bracket. (It's sometimes stocked by Pottery Barn.) Buy two, and mount them roughly at shoulder height so you can always see the tops of the flowers. Hang on either side of a picture or mirror. Keep the glass scrupulously clean (use bleach).

THE ART OF THE VIGNETTE

A long hallway that dead-ends at a blank wall is actually a design opportunity. Paint the wall a delicious color, and create a tableau against it. This will give you a focal point that tempers the lack of architectural interest. For example:

- Stand a shallow antique cabinet or small table against the end wall, and hang artwork above it.

- Buy three identically framed mirrors and hang them vertically on the end wall. Terry Trucco, the author of *Color: Details and Design* (PBC International), hung three large, round mirrors with plain black frames; they look like stacked portholes.

THE VICTORIAN SOLUTION

The Victorians were fond of bamboo and ebonized cabinets, which were not only elegant but often fairly shallow. Buy the largest you can afford, so that it will commandeer the hallway and turn it into a room of sorts. Arrange artwork over and around the cabinet.

UNIFY A DISPLAY

To tie together many disparate images that will hang in a hallway gallery, choose one type of frame—either black or gilt, suggests designer Barbara Southerland of New York and Greenville, NC. The frames need not match, but if their style and color are similar, then the images within them become kin as well.

THE COLLECTOR'S HALL

An instant collection of hallway-worthy photography can be ordered on-line from Corbis Store Fine Art & Photography. More than five hundred prints are available, including images by WPA photographer Dorothea Lange. To browse or purchase, visit their website (www.corbistore.com).

THE COLLECTOR'S HALL II

Fine-art photography from the 1930s and 1940s can also be found on-line from Timeless Traveler (www.timelesstraveler.com). Images by Ansel Adams, Walker Evans, Gordon Parks, and others are sold framed or in mats alone. A slim catalog is available; tel. (888) 321-2100.

UNDERSCORE A DOOR

Crown one or more doorways with an overdoor embellishment—an architectural wreath, swag, or fanciful bow in wood or plaster, from salvage yards or catalogs like Renovator's, Ballard Designs, and Outwater Plastics (see Chapter 6).

Make sure the flourish is in scale with the doorway; mock up the dimensions with blue masking tape before ordering, and trust your eye. Paint it white if it's new, but leave salvaged pieces alone; their patina is the signature of time.

OUT OF THE CLOSET

Make a frieze of great-looking hats, as design writer Terry Trucco did in the long front hallway of her apartment. She took six women's hats that were black or gray (so the collection would hold together visually) and hung them on long nails.

To make it work:

- Hang the hats high—roughly 6 inches below the picture railing or 12 to 18 inches below the ceiling. Use your judgment. If they're too low, the hall will feel narrower.

- Align the tops, not the bottoms, of the hats.

- Each hat should be a beauty in its own right. (This is not a storage system for baseball caps.) Beautiful 1940s hats of velvet and netting can still be had cheaply at thrift shops, as can Bogart-style fedoras.

- Don't crowd the hats. Tape them up with blue painter's tape until you get the composition right.

THE SHAKERESQUE HALL

A row of wooden Shaker pegs also makes a wonderful frieze. Hang the pegs high—perhaps 6 or 7 feet off the floor—and make them continuous, like molding. Every now and then, hang something from a peg; perhaps a hat here, a framed picture (suspended by a ribbon) there. Don't overdo it; the pegs, left bare, are both sculptural and historic.

Source: Shaker Workshops catalog (see Chapter 6).

THE ARTFUL ARRANGEMENT

Create a professional-looking grouping of pictures on the wall by first gathering them together on the floor. Move them around to get a visually pleasing arrangement. Then, to avoid pocking your walls with trial-and-error nail holes, try the following:

- Using scissors, tape, and clean paper, make paper "dummies" the exact size of each picture, and label each one.

- On each paper, mark where the wire will peak. (To do this, hold the actual picture by its wire, then measure from the wire's peak to the top of the frame.)

- Tape up the paper dummies to match the arrangement on your floor. Nail up Ook picture hooks (from hardware stores) right through the paper, matching *the bottom of the hook,* not the nail, to the mark you made on paper.

- Rip down one paper at a time and hang the appropriate picture.

*Tip: On plaster walls, nail over a piece of Scotch tape
so the plaster won't crumble. Leave tape in place.*

❧

ART WITHOUT A FRAME

If you have no terrific prints or gilt mirrors to hang in the hall, reconsider what constitutes art and hang what looks beautiful to you.

Old tools, easily found at country flea markets, can look sculptural and dramatic. Joseph Lembo and Laura Bohn, New York designers, built one client a ledge to hold sculptural cast-iron seats from vintage threshing machines. Hortensia Vitali, an Austin designer, once hung a lawn mower blade—a round metal object with shark's-tooth blades—from the 1940s. And New York designer Michael Buchanan painted a client's walls pumpkin, then hung an

Amish pitchfork and three antique hay hooks on the wall. "The tools cost less than $200," says Buchanan, "but by displaying them well, we elevated them into art objects."

Tip: If you have track lighting, use it well: spotlight the tools, not the center of the floor. Remember to have heavy objects hung by a contractor or carpenter.

FRAMES WITHOUT ART

A growing number of collectors are displaying antique frames on the wall—empty. Try hanging a small one within a larger one, as New York designer Cory Nicholas does.

UPGRADE THE FAMILY PHOTOS

For a client who wanted a hallway gallery of family photographs, New York designer Carl D'Aquino framed them so seriously that they suggest art, not snapshots. About seventy photos are identically framed in red lacquer with blue mats, and stacked six or seven high. "It's so joyful to walk through the hall," D'Aquino says.

Framing is no small expense, but visually it always pays off. A display like this one will look striking even if scaled down to far fewer pictures.

ANCESTOR PORTRAITS

Another way to enhance family photographs for hallway display is to have a photography shop reproduce them in sepia. "They're instant heirlooms," says New York designer Kim

DePole. "Even a tacky snapshot looks amazing in sepia."
Hang in groups—threes, fours, or more—as if you had plundered your great-grandmother's album.

*Tip: With a negative, you can have a sepia print made for about $1.
But for pictures where clarity is critical, have your photo scanned
into a computer; the cost may jump to $20, but in some cases
it may be worth the expense.*

❧

HALL OF MEMORIES

Design your own private gallery of handsomely framed mementos from people you care about: a card that came with roses years ago . . . a little watercolor from a friend's sketchbook . . . a love letter (brush it with tea to make it look old) . . . a handwritten poem. "It can be much more meaningful than prints or photographs," says Brooklyn designer Christopher Fox, "if it's an homage to someone you love." Remember, small items take on more importance when you scale up the size of the mat.

DRAW THE EYE UP

Hang a mirror or framed picture over the most important or prominent hallway door, and angle it down slightly so it will immediately engage your view. To angle a picture down, simply lower the wire so it's near the midpoint, not the top, of the frame.

THE ARCHITECTUAL FRAME

When arranging furniture or pictures in a hall, step back into the adjoining rooms and check your work from that perspective. Interior views can be jarring if they're off balance, so before making any arrangement permanent, take into account the natural frame created by each doorway. This is particularly important when your living or dining room offers a direct view of a hall.

HANG A FABRIC DOOR

In a hallway overcrowded with doorways, replace some of the doors with curtains, called *portieres*. Install a wooden curtain rod that's roughly 1 1/2 inches in diameter, cut to fit neatly inside the doorway. Paint it the color of your choice; brush on two coats of polyurethane for protection against scratches by curtain rings.

Hang a curtain of a rich material (velvet always looks good). Solid colors will contribute to a more pared-down look; patterns may only create visual clutter.

RUGS LIKE LILYPADS

Instead of buying a long, pricey runner for a long, narrow hall, shop flea markets and junque shops for smaller vintage rugs that you can array like stepping-stones.

This look thrives on Oriental designs with some age to them—as if you'd inherited a passel of rugs from a great-aunt. If they're matched in spirit and general size, their colors and patterns should harmonize.

Tip: Halls endure a lot of walking.
Put a pad under each rug to keep it anchored in place.

❦

CHAPTER 5

The
Surprisingly
Elegant
and Easy
Stairway

$\mathcal{M}$ ost people make the same mis-take with stairs as they do with ceilings: they don't address them at all," says Celeste Cooper, creative director of Repertoire, a design firm in Boston and New York. "But analyze what a staircase does, psychologically: you're leaving one level and ascending or descending to another. Will it be a ceremonial experience, or purely functional? Do you want the cleanest, crispest way of getting from one floor to another, or the most interesting?"

In other words, choose a mood. Serene. Passionate. Exotic. Zen. "Play with the space," urges Cooper. "You don't spend a lot of time here."

Restrictions are largely the sensible ones. Treads, or the part of the stair you step on, can't be slippery. The lighting must be decent. And given the height, leave papering or painting a staircase wall or ceiling to a professional.

Perhaps there is, in the end, one decorating cliché to avoid: the photo gallery of contemporary family photos, hung in ascending order. It's a predictable display, and that makes it, after a time, almost invisible. Family photos will thrive in a less spread out grouping and a more intimate space, and your stairway will be spared a decorating cliché.

Remember that a stairwell is inherently interesting. Its steps create a ziggurat pattern, and its height would be enviable in any other room. The slightest "extra"—a curve, a window, a beautiful color on the wall—is a splendid bonus. And even a dull staircase can be dramatized, as Cooper is quick to point out.

Neil Janovic, vice president of Janovic/Plaza Decorating Centers, offers his recipe for painting the various parts of a staircase—treads (the part you step on), risers (the vertical parts between the treads), railings, and balusters (the posts that hold the railing up):

- Sand, and prime with an acrylic undercoat.

- Follow with two coats of acrylic polyurethane enamel, a durable, water-based paint, in the color of your choice.

- Finish with two or three coats of clear, waterborne polyurethane. Use a high-gloss finish on a brightly painted banister railing, a less shiny satin or semigloss finish on other parts of the stair.

A note on paint: Some basic good advice and a strong caution appear in Chapter 1. Read before you paint.

DRAW THE EYE UP

To create interest and emphasize height in a staircase, designer Michael Buchanan of New York's Goralnick★ Buchanan likes wallpaper with a vertical tone-on-tone stripe. Like the stairs themselves, the stripes underscore the inherent drama of the two-story sweep of height. And tone-on-tone stripes look good in every color, from conservative ivory to Chinese red.

AN ENVELOPE OF COLOR

For an ordinary stairwell in a suburban house near Boston, Celeste Cooper "painted out" the undistinguished architecture and created a vivid composition of color. Walls, stairs, railings, even the adjoining foyer, were all painted with Benjamin Moore no. 1554, a brown-green-charcoal color that Cooper loves. "The dark color makes the stairwell dramatic and blanks out the shadows," she says.

Against that backdrop are dazzling—and essential—grace notes: a leopard-print runner, edged in red, and a shiny red banister railing. Now, instead of noticing an architecturally plain stairwell, a visitor is entranced by the ascending ribbons of red.

Cooper's red-stained banister railing was a custom job. For do-it-yourself painting tips, see the Janovic approach on page 79.

RECONSIDER THE BALUSTERS

Balusters—the vertical spindles that hold up the railing—can get scuffed over the years. Repaint them to match the walls.

To take some of the tedium out of painting round balusters, Neil Janovic recommends a specialized roller called a pipe roller or a Whizz round roller. To paint square balusters, use a sash painter (a paint pad on a handle) or a Whizz small roller, available at paint stores.

THE SKYLIT STAIR

If your staircase is brightened by a window, bring the outdoors in by painting the stairway ceiling sky blue or robin's-egg blue, just as the Victorians treated their porch ceilings. Three historically correct blues from color expert Kenneth X. Charbonneau: Benjamin Moore nos. 765, 757, and 751.

Tip: Unless there is an architectural boundary, you'll probably need to carry the blue paint across the entire upstairs hall ceiling.

❦

HOW GREEN IS MY STAIRCASE

For a client who lived in the country, the legendary decorator Sister Parish painted the treads (the flat parts, for stepping on) and risers (the vertical sections between the treads) leaf-green, then had an artist paint vine-entwined railings along the wall. Decorative painting is an investment, but it's well worth the money to bring magic to a small space.

*Tip: If you live near a good art school, talk to the employment office:
it can put you in touch with recent graduates
who may have good work in their portfolios,
and at reasonable prices. Always request a sketch in advance.*

❧

THE ANTIQUE STAIR

Old-house stairways can reveal their age in subtle ways. Sometimes they run narrow, or their treads are worn down in the middle from a century or so of use. This kind of age creates the perfect setting for a historic wallpaper, such as the intricate nature-based patterns by the English Arts and Crafts designer William Morris. If you have trouble choosing one, try Willow, a classic paper that flatters any space it graces.

Source: Bradbury & Bradbury's famous catalog (about $12) is big, beautiful, and packed with swatches. Contact the company at P.O. Box 155, Benicia, CA 94510; tel. (707) 746-1900, or e-mail info@bradbury.com. A few examples are posted at www.bradbury.com.

THE WELL-TRODDEN STAIR

If you're wedded to farmhouse style, try painting your stairs white and adjusting your attitude so you welcome the signs of wear. Boston designers Cheryl and Jeffrey Katz painted their town house stairs with ordinary wall paint—Benjamin Moore's Linen White latex, in a satin finish—applying two coats and no protective sealer. "We don't care that it gets scuffed," says Cheryl. "It truly looks old, but it's our way of having a little country in the city."

ASCENDING COLORS

For handsome staircase graphics, run a low-key rainbow, comprising shades of just one color, up the steps. Start at the bottom with the darkest hue and work your way up to the lightest, aiming for subtle differences rather than stark contrasts. To get it right, collect a fistful of paint strips from the paint store, snip them up into individual color samples, and rearrange until you're pleased with the results.

POUR ON THE LIGHT

Many stairwells are starved for light. Ann Kale, a New York lighting designer, has successfully lighted stairs for dozens of clients using either of these options:

- Hang a chandelier or pendant (hanging) light. Center it over the entire stairwell, not over the steps. If you can see bare bulbs from below, make them no higher than 40 watts each. Finally, hang the fixture so that its bottom is roughly 6 feet higher than the top stair landing. "The height depends on the proportions of the stairwell," says Kale. Before calling the electrician, she advises, "Try doing an illustration to scale, and see what height looks best."

- Install two wall sconces along each flight of stairs—or, if the landings are in shadow, install a sconce on each landing and a third over the stairs. Center it about 6 feet above a tread.

Tip: In a traditional home, Kale says, use incandescent bulbs. For modern interiors with cool colors or white walls, try halogen fixtures instead.

❧❀❧

CLAIM THE EMPTY SPACE

"The greatest thing going in a stairwell is the height," says Chicago interior designer Janet Schirn. "Use it!" She hangs textiles, antique or otherwise, so they float over the stairs like banners (perpendicular to the walls) from wooden dowels or metal rods. Let the heights of the banners ascend with the steps. "You can also hang a series of architectural box kites, or exquisite dragon kites," she suggests.

Tip: The rods can hang from nylon filament (fishing line) or slender chains attached to hooks in the ceiling; have the installation done by a carpenter or contractor.

❧❀❧

A DRIZZLE OF LANTERNS

If you have access to decorative Chinese paper lanterns, hang a dozen or more over the stairs, as if they were raining down. (The lowest height for a lantern would be 6½ feet over a particular step; others could hang higher, filling the empty space.) The lanterns, meant to hang empty, come in reds, yellows, and white; aim for a dazzling mix of color, like fireworks, or the Zenlike simplicity of all white.

For lanterns, shop markets in your local Chinese neighborhood, or visit the website of Pearl River Mart, a New York emporium: www.pearlriver.com. (Click on "Our Products," then on "Home Furnishings.")

THE LUXURIOUS LANDING

A stair landing with a window is a found room in miniature, worth exploiting. If you have the staggering good fortune to have a decent-size landing, add a skinny bench and a cigarette table, just big enough for a book. You may not spend much time there, but it sets a hospitable scene

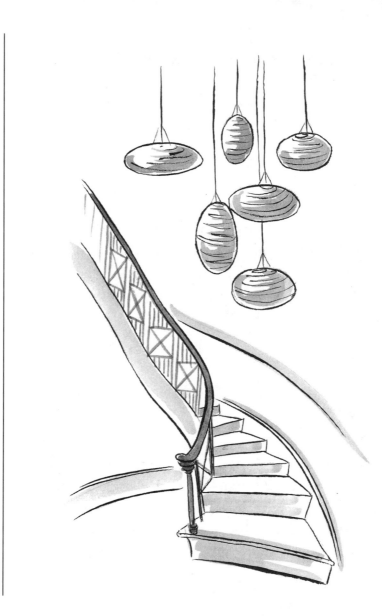

(and, given enough daylight, may even become a reading nook).

Or hint at the garden by setting a piece of antique stone statuary or a pitted stone birdbath near the window.

Tip: Be particularly careful around stairs—don't set objects where they might trip someone in the dark or be pulled over by a child.

꧁꧂

THE STAIRWAY GALLERY

When hanging art in a stairwell, stagger it on the wall so it reiterates the steps. Some tips to guide you:

- "Get out the yardstick," says designer Barbara Southerland. The distance between each step and the lowest picture in your arrangement should hold constant as you ascend.

- Don't hang oil paintings on a stairwell; this is a place of transition, not contemplation. Do hang prints, drawings, watercolors, even an evolving collection of your child's art (as long as it's seriously framed).

• Make the lowest picture at shoulder height. Then stack at least two high—straight up to the ceiling, if desired. (If you don't stack at least two pictures above each step,

the arrangement will look thin, particularly under that high ceiling.) As for the the highest pieces, you'll see them clearly from the second floor.

THE ANCESTRAL STAIRWAY

Sometimes it looks stilted to line a stairway with recent color photos of family members. But *ancestral* family photos in sepia or black and white are another matter: each suggests a story, and imparts a secretive whiff of the past. For impact, frame them with oversize mats—a minimum of 4 inches wide on each side. Gather enough to create a real grouping.

THE WELL-CARPETED STAIR

For a classic, can't-go-wrong stair runner, try Barbara Southerland's favorite: a plain black runner with a patterned border. Just make sure, Southerland advises, that there's a touch of black in the pattern as well, so that the pattern and border look related. "Tie it into your foyer by using a similar rug there, too," she suggests.

THE WELL-CARPETED STAIR II

Fur patterns, from leopard to delicate spotted fawn, make gorgeous stair runners. (For high drama, try zebra.) Have a solid black border applied, or simply paint the stair treads black.

THE ALL-NATURAL STAIR

Coir, a rug material made of coconut fibers, is a durable cousin of sisal that looks good and wears well on stairs. (Like sisal, it can't be cleaned, just vacuumed, so it works best in dog-free and child-free homes.) Some tips from ABC Carpet & Home, the New York rug emporium:

Buy a tightly woven coir, as loose weaves are a trap for high heels. Have the border, if you want one, professionally applied; it will be glued to the edges of the coir. You might also consider wool sisal, which can be professionally cleaned. Just don't choose sea grass for stairs; though some designers love it, it can prove fragile—and slippery.

LONG LIVE THE RUNNER

Even the most expensive wool runners will wear out at the "nose," or the front edge of each step, cautions Mark Saley at ABC Carpet. Indeed, you can expect to replace nearly any runner after two to three years, he says—unless you use his life-prolonging trick:

Order enough carpeting so your installer can cut a few extra slices for you to save. When the carpeting starts showing wear at the nose of the steps, have the installer come back and hoist the entire runner a few inches higher, using the slice to fill in at the base of the stairs. The wear will be evenly distributed, and your runner may last twice as long.

A VERY TALL MURAL

In an eighteenth-century-style house, New York designer Carl D'Aquino painted a vertical mural on the risers of the steps; looking up, a visitor perceives the entire picture, not just the individual "slices." The mural began with an artist's drawing (on paper) of a rural scene, its houses and trees and green hills reaching as high as all the risers combined. The paper was then cut apart so that each slice could be copied, in artist's paint, onto the risers. Of course, a photograph or painting could be copied onto the stairs as well. "You just ignore the horizontal treads," D'Aquino says.

This is a job for a muralist—a trade listed in the Yellow Pages, incidentally. (Always look at the artist's work first.) If your staircase is prominently positioned, the glorious results may justify the investment.

THE ARTISTIC STAIR

Indulge in just a roll or two of an exquisite hand-printed wallcovering—not for the walls, but to paper the risers of your stairs. Seal with several coats of matte polyurethane so scuff marks can be wiped away.

Tip: Your papered risers will truly stand out if the walls are painted a solid color.

❧❀❧

THE TUXEDO STAIR

As a general rule of thumb, treads (the part you step on) should be darker than risers (the vertical part of a stair). The Chicago designer Richar suggests mahogany-stained treads and white-painted risers as a classical and elegant combination, along with a mahogany-stained rail.

If it's not practical to strip and stain the stairs, use paint instead: white risers, black treads. Paint the rail shiny black to match the treads.

IGNITE A SHINE OVERHEAD

To make the most of a stairway's height, Richar tends to the ceiling, often applying squares of imitation silver or gold leaf until the entire ceiling is covered. It's the labor, not the leaf, that's expensive, but if you are redecorating a home you plan to keep, this extraordinary touch is worth considering.

Tip: For a shortcut, use wallpaper that mimics the effect of gold or silver leaf.

THE WITTY STAIR

New York designer Jeffrey Bilhuber once had a stair runner custom-woven with an ascending pattern of dog's paws, as if the client's dog had stepped in mud before bounding up the stairs. For a do-it-yourself version, handpaint your own dog, cat, or bird tracks (try light gray tracks on black stairs, or black tracks on white stairs—no rules govern this kind of playfulness). You need not be an artist; simply adapt the tracks from a real-life example, and practice on paper first.

THE WITTY STAIR II

Another Bilhuber inspiration is to hire a decorative artist to paint a trompe l'oeil dollar bill on a stairway landing. "We would watch people try to pick it up," he wryly recalls. This effect does require an artist or muralist, but it's not a big investment. You can try a similar artistic trick with the painted image of a postcard or letter, theater tickets, or an engraved invitation.

THE MOST FLATTERING COLOR

Use shades of peach to bring out the beauty of a graceful staircase. (Peach walls are also flattering to the skin.) Paint the walls Benjamin Moore no. 150, the color of marzipan, suggests Joan Malter Osburn, a San Francisco designer. For an adjacent foyer or hall, use Benjamin Moore no. 151, a slightly darker hue.

REMEMBER THE DECORATIVE DETAILS

If you have a stair runner, pay attention to the stair rods, which hold it in place and serve as jewelry for the staircase. With a patterned runner, plain brass rods will do, since they'll barely be noticed. But with solid-color runners, suggests New York designer Marshall Watson, consider wrought-iron or glass rods.

DIGNIFY A HUMDRUM STAIR

If you live in a house of three stories or more, your stairwell probably loses some of its width and stature after the first flight. Upgrade it by giving it the same decorative treatment

as on the first floor, establishing continuity with the same (or related) carpet and paint or wallpaper—even hanging related pictures on the wall. The sense of continuity can make your house feel larger and more cohesive.

LET THE CURVES SEDUCE

The curve of a staircase can enfold, at its base, a seemingly useless bit of floor space. Don't ignore it—use it to indulge a fantasy.

The tea-for-one fantasy. New York designer David Barrett put a diminutive round table with a single chair under the snail-shell curve of his stair. He even installed a tiny downlight in the underside of the stair, lighting the tabletop.

The secret hideaway fantasy. If your curved stair has a scoop of space beneath it, try "furnishing" it with large floor pillows, perhaps covered in raw silk. If desired, add a telephone. Heaven.

The Architectural Digest *fantasy.* Buy a pedestal shaped like a pillar (try flea markets and antique shops) and set it on the floor so the stair curves around it. Place a potted orchid on top; it looks expensive (and may easily cost $50 or so), but the exotic blossoms can last many weeks.

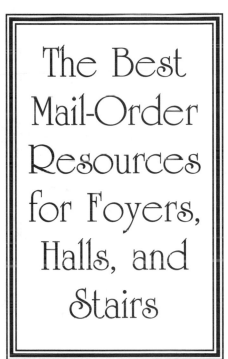

The Best
Mail-Order
Resources
for Foyers,
Halls, and
Stairs

This resource list includes the quirky as well as the classic. Catalog prices do change, so they're not included here—but many of these are free.

Anthropologie
One Margaret Way
Ridgely, MD 21685
(800) 309-2500
www.anthropologie.com

Amid the clothes and furnishings are some wonderful reproductions for foyers and halls, such as a copy of a 1920s French bistro coat rack with mirror, and various hooks, ledges, and display brackets.

Ballard Designs
1670 DeFoor Avenue N.W.
Atlanta, GA 30318
(800) 367-2775

A superb selection of skinny shelving and picture ledges that seem made for a narrow hall. Also wall sconces, narrow console tables, architectural embellishments such as overdoor ornaments, shallow curio cabinets to hang on the wall, mirrors, and 10-foot-long runners of stenciled jute.

The Bright Spot
33 Chestnut Street
Westmont, IL 60559
Tel. (800) 736-0126
Fax (800) 736-1329

Copies and adaptations of Arts and Crafts lighting, from a brass sconce inspired by Frank Lloyd Wright to a Tiffany design called Spider (described, when unlighted, as "a deliciously sinister masterpiece of dark brooding power").

Calico Corners
203 Gale Lane
Kennett Square, PA 19348
(800) 213-6366

A beautiful catalog of fabrics (yard-long swatches are available on loan) and furnishings, custom-covered with your choice of material. The slender, upholstered benches are well sized for a foyer, hall, or generous stair landing.

Craftsman Homes Connection
2525 East 29th Street, Suite 10B-343
Spokane, WA 99223
(509) 535-5098
www.crafthome.com

Browse on-line, if you can; the website has audio on some pages, so you can hear the doorbells chime and the restored telephones ring. All objects are faithful to the

Arts and Crafts style: doorbells, door knockers, welcome mats, Mission-style mirrors, beautiful switchplates, and antique-style push-button and toggle switches.

Crate & Barrel
P.O. Box 3200
Naperville, IL 60566
(800) 323-5461
   Framed mirrors, runners, tables, and accessories, very simple and classic.

Design Toscano
1645 Greenleaf Avenue
Elk Grove Valley, IL 60007
(800) 525-0733
   Amid the cast gargoyles are a few pieces that seem made for halls or foyers, such as a wrought-iron candle sconce, a decorative frieze in the style of Louis Sullivan, and a replica of a stunning antique French urn.

Elements
P.O. Box 6105
Rapid City, SD 57709
(800) 778-5555
   A lithe but well-edited catalog from Spiegel that includes benches, small tables, side chairs, frames, unusual rugs, and accessories.

Exposures Homes
P.O. Box 3615
Oshkosh, WI 54903
(800) 699-6993
   Benches, side tables, side chairs, vases, frames, mirrors, and other pieces, all stylish and simple.

*The Best
Mail-Order
Resources for
Foyers, Halls,
and Stairs*
105

Gardeners Eden
17 Riverside Street
Nashua, NH 03062
(800) 822-9600

Quite a few indoor furnishings: benches, chests, cabinets, lithe metal chairs, indoor fountains, even a hall mirror with hooks for scarves and keys.

Garnet Hill
231 Main Street
Franconia, NH 03580
(800) 622-6216

Known for bedding, Garnet Hill also offers rugs and runners. Some are hand-hooked, some are inspired by antique rugs or Amish quilts.

Hold Everything
P.O. Box 7807
San Francisco, CA 94120
(800) 421-2264

Wooden hangers in several styles—the finishing detail for every hall closet—along with storage boxes designed to hold papers but perfect on closet shelves for gloves and scarves.

IKEA
8352 Honeygo Boulevard
Baltimore, MD 21236
(800) 434-IKEA
www.ikea.com

Side chairs, framed mirrors, wooden hangers, armoires and shelving, lighting, rugs, display ledges and clocks . . . and more.

Illuminations
1995 South McDowell Boulevard
Petaluma, CA 94954
(800) CANDLES
    A wide and sensual assortment of candles, from tapers and pillar candles to the
Rituals Candles formulated to promote (or at least invoke) qualities like abundance,
love, happiness, protection, and forgiveness.

Kate's Paperie
561 Broadway
New York, NY 10012
(800) 809-9880
    Exotic sheets of handmade paper (consult a paperhanger about affixing to walls).
Here are handmade papers seeded with bits of mulberry bark, or laced with silver, or
embedded with leaves of grass and rose petals. For more ideas, consult the book
Paperie, by Kate's Paperie with Bo Niles (Simon & Schuster).

Legacy
514 North Third Street
Minneapolis, MN 55401
(800) 328-2711
    Every three months, Legacy comes out with another themed catalog—lodge style,
for example, or Swedish style. Watch for rugs, chairs, lamps, framed photographs,
mirrors, sconces, and storage pieces.

Lehman's Non-Electric Catalog
One Lehman Circle, P.O. Box 41
Kidron, OH 44636
(330) 857-5757
www.lehmans.com
    The catalog that sells gas-powered refrigerators to the Amish also stocks pure
beeswax candles, handmade soaps, and gorgeous Victorian metal brackets (called

*The Best
Mail-Order
Resources for
Foyers, Halls,
and Stairs*

107

"bracket lamps") to hold pillar candles or small gas lamps. Add the silvery glass re-
flector if you want to magnify the light.

Martha By Mail
P.O. Box 60060
Tampa, FL 33660
(800) 950-7130
www.marthastewart.com
  You have to mine this catalog carefully to find accessories for foyers and halls, but
it's worth it. Martha offers candles in delicate pastels, wirework holders for flowers
and postcards, soaps for the powder room, mirrors, and more.

Mig and Tig Furniture
549 North Wells
Chicago, IL 60610
(312) 644-8277
  Cast-iron candle sconces; the occasional mirror and console table.

Museum of Modern Art
Mail Order Department
11 West 53rd Street
New York, NY 10019
(800) 447-6662
  This edgy collection includes the Bookworm, a flexible, even curvaceous book-
shelf that hangs on the wall; at just 8 inches deep, it won't intrude on a narrow hall.
For foyers, note the colorful coat rack designed in 1953 by Charles and Ray Eames.

The Natural Choice
1365 Rufina Circle
Santa Fe, NM 87505
(800) 621-2591
  Nontoxic and natural stains, paints, and other products, worth considering for
every part of the home.

Outwater Plastics Industries
4 Passaic Street, P.O. Drawer 403
Wood-Ridge, NJ 07075
(888) OUTWATER
www.outwater.com

   Almost as large as a telephone book, this dry-looking industrial catalog has a few choice finds for foyers and halls, especially toward the back. Note the plasterlike wall niches, pilasters (flat columns to run down a long hall), urns, display brackets, and pressed-metal ornaments, like suns and fleurs-de-lis.

Pottery Barn
P.O. Box 7044
San Francisco, CA 94120
(800) 922-5507

   Affordable rugs and runners, pendant lighting, window treatments, small shelves and display ledges, mirrors, telephone tables, wall vases, and many other items for foyers and halls.

Renovator's
P.O. Box 2515
Conway, NH 03818-2515
(800) 659-2211

   Embossed English wallpapers and borders, plaster-look Victorian wall and ceiling medallions.

Restoration Hardware
104 Challenger Drive
Portland, TN 37148
(800) 762-1005

   Small tables, lighting, framed archival photographs, quirky accessories (a gleaming doorstop shaped like a jack), and Silver Sage paint, the exact shade of green used in the firm's stores—call for a swatch.

*The Best
Mail-Order
Resources for
Foyers, Halls,
and Stairs*

109

Room
151 West 30th Street, Suite 705
New York, NY 10001
(888) 420-ROOM

Framed mirrors and small hallway-appropriate furnishings, such as benches and consoles, all with a hip modern sensibility. A collection of custom photography is in the works. Room looks like a sleek design magazine—except that everything on its pages is for sale.

Shaker Workshops
P.O. Box 8001
Ashburnham, MA 01430
(800) 840-9121
www.shakerworkshops.com

Many items in this catalog have lost their Shakeresque simplicity, but the rest are still noteworthy. For foyers and halls, consider the blanket boxes, pegboard and pegged shelves, benches and settees, side chairs, mirrors, and clocks.

Smith & Hawken Home & Clothing
2 Arbor Lane, Box 6900
Florence, KY 41022
(800) 776-3336
www.smith-hawken.com

A narrow but refined selection of console tables, lighting, and decorative accessories, from console tables through clocks to pear-shaped candles.

Smith+Noble Windoware
P.O. Box 1838
Corona, CA 91718
(800) 248-8888

If you're willing to do your own measuring and installation, here are classic blinds and draperies at a healthy discount. For a foyer or stairwell, where absolute privacy is not required, shades of natural materials—bamboo, rattan, and others—allow sunlight to slip inside.

Spiegel
P.O. Box 182555
Columbus, OH 43218
(800) 345-4500
   A pricey ($10) catalog that's worth its weight in console tables, framed mirrors, candle sconces and clocks, diminutive tables, runners, and window treatments.

The Stencil Collector
1723 Tilghman Street
Allentown, PA 18104
(610) 433-2105
   A great selection of architectural stencils, from urns and balustrades to arches and pillars; all can add character to a foyer, hall, or staircase wall.